Why Are Americans Obsessed with Guns And Willing to Pay A High Price for Them?

M. Basheer Ahmed M.D.

WHY ARE AMERICANS OBSESSED WITH GUNS AND WILLING TO PAY A HIGH PRICE FOR THEM?
Copyright © 2022 by M. Basheer Ahmed M.D.

All rights reserved. No part of this publication may be reproduced, distributed, or transmitted in any form or by any means, including photocopying, recording, or other electronic or mechanical methods, without the prior written permission of the publisher or author, except in the case of brief quotations embodied in critical reviews and certain other noncommercial uses permitted by copyright law.

Although every precaution has been taken to verify the accuracy of the information contained herein, the author and publisher assume no responsibility for any errors or omissions. No liability is assumed for damages that may result from the use of information contained within.

Library of Congress Control Number: 2022903242
ISBN-13:   Paperback: 978-1-64749-646-3
           Epub: 978-1-64749-647-0

Printed in the United States of America

GoToPublish LLC
1-888-337-1724
www.gotopublish.com
info@gotopublish.com

This book is dedicated to all the young people who lost their lives due to gun violence and never had the opportunity to become great leaders, scholars, or scientists.

ACKNOWLEDGEMENT

I would like to thank my son Sameer Ahmed for reviewing this manuscript and for his helpful suggestions.

CONTENTS

Foreword 7
Preface 13
Introduction 19
Mass Shootings in the United States 23
Why Do Americans Have an Obsession About
    Possessing Guns?... 28
Gun Violence Is an Epidemic 32
Mental Illness Suicide and Death by Gun Violence...... 38
Gun Violence is Killing More Children 46
The Second Amendment and Individuals' Right
    to Bear Arms 49
Congress Inhibits Research Proposals Related to
    Causes and Effects of Firearm Violence 54
The NRA and Lawmakers 60
Controlling Gun Violence 66
Conclusion 70

FOREWORD

Michael Ross M.D.

A child finds and plays with a loaded handgun and inadvertently kills a sibling. An angry husband shoots his spouse in a fit of rage. A minor fender bender escalates into "road rage" and a shooting. Anger at a lost job, bigotry or misogynistic prejudices too frequently lead to deaths of multiple innocent individuals. This pattern of gun deaths is much more common in the United States than elsewhere in the developed world. In the United States, there are more firearms than people.

My friend, Dr. M. Basheer Ahmed M.D., takes an in depth look in this volume at the reasons behind gun deaths in the United States. Dr. Ahmed is uniquely qualified for this difficult task. As a practicing Psychiatrist for over fifty years, he has spent decades analyzing, counseling, and helping victims of all sorts of physical or psychologic stress and violence. Dr. Ahmed has published book-length studies about domestic violence. He also brings a distinctive perspective to analysis of U.S. gun ownership and bloodshed having been born, raised, and educated outside the U.S., immigrating to the United States after his Psychiatry fellowship at renowned British medical centers.

Does Dr. Ahmed answer all the questions, provide reasons for widespread gun violence, and offer politically workable solutions? Perhaps as well as can be postulated in the current partisan and social climate. At a minimum, after one reads, studies, and analyzes this volume, the reader will be left with a more information, a more critical understanding of the issues, and some insight into the human psych explained by a truly talented and caring physician. I heartily recommend carefully studying the reasons Dr. Ahmed gives for Americans' obsession for possessing guns resulting in the highest gun ownership per capita in the world. He also persuasively endorses the need for public education by religious leaders of all faiths, educators, and health professionals, to change public opinion which can influence the legislators to support the much-needed laws supporting responsible gun ownership.

Michael Ross M.D.
Past President of Congregation Beth El, Fort Worth, TX, and a national trustee of the Union of Reform Judaism

Dr. Basheer Ahmed has written a necessary, but disturbing look at a central feature and major problem of American life…namely, the epidemic known as gun violence.

In a human rights context, every person, according to article 1 of the Universal Declaration of Human Rights, is entitled to a life with dignity and rights. Due to the ongoing, and tragically seemingly never-ending scourge of gun violence, tens of thousands of innocent lives are cut short due to the irresponsible and bipartisan failure to make any meaningful changes in gun laws.

With an average of 40,000 lives a year lost to gun violence, there is simply no way of telling the human loss to society… how many of the victims, especially juveniles/children, might have grown up to be future leaders in their communities, states, and the country, only to see their families plunged into grief due to their unnatural deaths at the hands of someone with a gun?

What is wrong with this picture?? Most everything. Dr. Ahmed's stinging assessment should be a wakeup call for anyone with a conscience to demand political change on this issue, or to be the spark to encourage many to simply run for office themselves to ensure that gun laws change.

Society has a right to be protected, and human beings have a right and a moral duty to have the opportunity to live a life with dignity. This work should jolt anyone who is fed up with the societal disease of violence into constructive action… immediately.

Professor Rick Halperin
Director, Southern Methodist University
Human Rights program
Dallas Texas

The issue of gun violence is one that is of high concern to our society. It affects all citizens of our country.

In his paper on the subject, Dr. Basheer Ahmed, a former professor of psychiatry and human rights activist, examines the issue from a historical and clinical perspective.

Dr. Basheer's analysis is crucial to developing local and national gun safety policies. His arguments are thorough, and cogent and, if adopted by policy makers, will help us as we attempt to stem the plague of gun violence that plagues our society.

I recommend that Dr. Basheer's work be read by scholars, students, activists, and elected officials. Digesting it and implementing its recommendations will benefit our society and those who reside in it.

Dr. Lee P. Brown
Former Mayor and Chief of Police of Houston Texas.

I am writing in support of the excellent booklet by Basheer Ahmed M.D., which states, *"If we're going to curb gun violence, we must first dismantle a national obsession."*

My reading of this booklet comes on the heels of a school shooting here in Tarrant County, where a young man felt so cornered that he had no other options other than to bring a gun to school to defend himself from his bullies. It also comes on the heels of the verdict of the trial, where a jury decided that he acted in self-defense when he used an AR-15 style semi-automatic rifle to shoot three people.

While many Americans can agree that these cases are steeped in emotion, in sometimes not knowing the full story, and in folks deciding what a "just" cause is for shooting someone, one thing is clear: these are issues which plague us because there is such a prevalence and accessibility to guns. Both of these cases involve teenagers having access to firearms. Both of these cases involve someone bringing a firearm into a crowded situation specifically because they felt they may have no other recourse.

We must do better as a country. We must help our citizens feel safe and also feel heard without the use of firearms. We must get weapons of war out of civilian circulation. We must put a stop to divisive rhetoric which drives people to feel so afraid or so emboldened that they find firearms to be their only recourse. This will take significant active effort on the part of the American people.

There is much work to do. Your booklet outlines some excellent steps for how to achieve a reduction in gun violence in the United States. I look forward to encouraging readers from all walks of life to learn from your expertise.

Allison Campolo, Ph.D.
Tarrant County Democratic Party Chair

PREFACE

M. Basheer Ahmed, MD.

I have been practicing psychiatry in the United States since 1968. During the last three decades, I saw survivors and families of gun violence. Statistics tells us that over 40,000 people are killed each year by gun violence, and hundreds of thousands of people are injured. However, the effect of gun violence is far beyond these figures because the survivors and the families of the victims who suffered the consequences are not counted in this statistic. If we take into account the sufferings of the families, then the figures can rise to half a million per year.

I have not witnessed any mass shooting or even death by gun, but the experience I have counseling the survivors and families makes me aware of the sufferings these people experience. Unfortunately, the United States has the highest number of gun violence per capita in the world.

Imagine the hundreds of thousands of children and their families affected by the mass shootings in Columbine

High School in 1999, Sandy Hook Elementary School in Connecticut, Marjory Stoneman High School in Florida, Oxford High School in Michigan, and countless other school shootings. These survivors and families suffer from post-traumatic stress disorder (PTSD), which causes anxiety and depression. Some of the patients suffer for years. In fact, one student from Marjory Stoneman High School killed himself after suffering for two years with PTSD.

The trauma that the teachers experienced have debilitating effects as well. In addition to difficulty returning to work, the teachers also experience frustration that their concerns about the students' behaviors are not resulting in appropriate action by administration. As it happened, in Oxford High School in Michigan, a teacher notified the school about the unusual behavior of the student, but no action was taken. The 15-year-old child brought a gun given by his parents to school. He killed four students.

The parents of young children have a tough time explaining why somebody is shooting at young children and what can be done. How will the children think about their schools- as a place of learning or as a place of danger? Parents express their frustration at not knowing if their school-aged child will experience any such tragedy.

Death due to gun violence was not reduced during the pandemic of 2020-2021. In fact, it increased, due to a rise in intimate partner violence and an increase in purchases of guns.

We hear loud and clear the right to own guns and carry a gun wherever and whenever we want. Shouldn't we also consider the right of people to live peacefully, shop in the mall, visit a movie theater, or attend school safely?

Why do Americans have the highest incidence of death due to gun violence compared to any part of the industrialized world? Since I was actively involved in treating some of the survivors and the families of the victims, I engaged in searching for the causes and solutions.

I wrote this article based on my own conclusions about the causes for the American obsession with gun ownership and recommend an entirely different approach to controlling this deadly menace.

In the summer of 2019 more than 26 mass shootings gripped the United States: in May, a disgruntled worker entered a Virginia Beach municipal building and fatally shot twelve people; in August, a 21-year-old was accused of massacring nearly two dozen shoppers at a Walmart in El Paso; the next day, a gunman opened fire on a crowded street in downtown Dayton, Ohio, killing nine.

The survivors of those horrific tragedies whose pleas for change and legislative action to keep guns out of the hands of potentially dangerous people have fallen on deaf ears.

Just before the deadly shooting in El Paso, Governor Greg Abbott signed ten pro-gun bills into law, which made it easier for Texans to buy military-style arsenals for self-defense, like those soldiers use to fight in hostile countries. It is not simply anger or any other motivation that is the real problem. It is the easy availability of a gun which kills people.

According to national statistics, guns cause over 40,000 deaths and 100,000 injuries per year. Over 22,000 people commit suicide, homicides take another 13,000 lives. The level of gun violence in the US is one of the highest in the world, with 4.43 deaths per 100,000 people. That is nine times the rate in Canada, which has 0.47 deaths per 100,000 people. In those countries where gun violence is higher than in the United States—in particular in Central and South America and the Caribbean—it is due to the presence of gangs related to drug trafficking. Of the world's annual 251,000-gun deaths, more than half of them occur in six countries—Brazil, Mexico, Columbia, Venezuela, Guatemala, and the United States.

A major reason for the United States' high death rate from guns is due to gun ownership and the weak laws governing it. According to recent estimates, 400 million guns are owned by the United States public. People own one to multiple guns per capita in the United States. The United States does not have more crime than other developed countries, but it does have more lethal violence due to the access to guns.

With the inauguration of the new president, we have reason to be cautiously optimistic. President Joseph R. Biden rightfully characterizes gun violence in the United States as a "public health epidemic." In the early 1990s, during his tenure in the U.S. Senate, Biden helped pass the Brady Handgun Violence Prevention Act as well as a 10-year ban on assault weapons and high-capacity magazines in 1994.

A recent poll by the Pew Research Center revealed that 79 percent of Republicans favored protecting gun ownership rights over imposing limitations to gun access.

The Second Amendment protects the use of weapons for lawful purposes only, including self-defense. Rapid-fire weapons, machine guns, and similar weapons of mass destruction may be useful in war, but I can't imagine the framers of the Constitution imagined civilians roaming about with machine guns during peace time.

Nonetheless, owning guns like these remains an obsession for countless Americans. Look no further than the 17-year-old accused of gunning down three people (killing two of them) at a Black Lives Matter demonstration in Kenosha this summer. The gun he was brandishing? A military-style, semi-automatic AR-15.

Religious leaders from Christian, Jewish, Muslim, Sikh, and Hindu communities shared the impact of gun violence based on years of experience counseling the victims and their families. They spoke against the gun violence plaguing their communities as they have witnessed the grave impact that gun violence has on families, schools, houses of worship, and neighborhoods.

Even corporate America has spoken in favor of strong measures for gun control. Dick's Sporting Goods overhauled its gun sales policies, stopped selling guns in two hundred of its new stores, and destroyed about $5 million worth of weapons, turning them into scrap metal. Dick's also pulled all military-style weapons from its stores, banned high-capacity magazines, and will not sell firearms to anyone under the age of twenty-one.

Edward Stack, Dick's CEO, publicly criticized Senate Majority Leader Mitch McConnell for withholding gun control legislation in Congress. Not surprisingly, the National Rifle Association (NRA), Republican lawmakers, and customers chastised Stack for his sensible decisions. Yet, Mr. Stack set an example for other gun sellers to put saving lives above bottom-line profits.

In 2015, the American College of Physicians (ACP) joined fifty-two health organizations to address gun violence as a public health threat. The recommendations include encouraging physicians to discuss with patients the risks associated with keeping a firearm in the home along with methods for mitigating the risk. The ACP also strongly recommends the sale of firearms be subject to completion of an educational program on firearm safety, universal background checks, banning assault weapons with large-capacity magazines, closing the gun show loophole (private sales at gun shows), and prosecuting people who sell firearms illegally or purchase firearms for anyone banned from gun possession (straw purchases).

There is an abundant need for public education in the United States about gun violence, regulating gun sales, closing loopholes in existing laws, and implementing a nationwide gun licensing system. It is our responsibility as citizens to make people aware of the consequences of gun obsession and ineffective gun laws. Because our knowledge of human behavior is not advanced enough to predict behavior — nor is it reasonable that every purchaser receives a certification from a behavioral scientist to buy a gun — public education is the best way we have to change the behavior. I strongly encourage physicians, clergy, and teachers to take responsibility for educating the public about the dangers of owning a gun, the impact they have on innocent victims, and the traumatic effects gun violence has on thousands of survivors.

These three groups—health professionals, faith leaders, and schools and colleges—have access to most people living in the United States. They are compassionate, care for and value human life, and are concerned about the high incidence of death from gun violence.

I strongly recommend that all organizations that support gun control add a robust public education component to their mission. I am confident we can control the epidemic of gun violence if we intervene early in a young person's life by insisting health professions, faith leaders, and teachers do their part to challenge the unexamined assumptions that for too long have governed the rationale for gun ownership in America.

INTRODUCTION

I was five years old the first time I saw a gun.
Growing up in Hyderabad, India, the only times I even really heard guns discussed were in conversations about hunting. My family was visiting a relative, an avid deer hunter, when I took note of the unloaded rifle hanging on the wall and safely out of reach.

Even in the eyes of a child, the sight of the gun alone was insignificant. A gun was merely a tool for hunters, I'd always been taught. You see, gun violence—particularly mass-casualty shootings—is virtually nonexistent in India. Never before had I heard of a gun used as a weapon to commit murder.

The cultural attitudes surrounding guns in my native India have their origins, at least in part, rooted in legislation (the Arms Act of 1959 and the Arms Rules in 1962) stipulating that a person could not own a gun unless they could prove they feared for their safety or the safety of their families. It's a far cry from the reality I have come to know.

Besides the one relative from my childhood or those who were military, I never knew anyone who owned a gun.

WHY ARE AMERICANS OBSESSED WITH GUNS AND WILLING TO PAY A HIGH PRICE FOR THEM?

In January 1968, I landed in the country of my dreams after completing my post-graduate studies in psychiatry at Glasgow University, Scotland. I became fascinated with the United States as a teenager after visiting the U.S. Information Center in my hometown of Hyderabad, India.

I was impressed by how immigrants of diverse cultures, religions, ethnicity, and languages came from all over the world and lived together in peace and harmony in the United States. I learned that in this country of opportunity, people could pursue their goals and actualize their dreams.

During the 1960s, when I was studying in the United Kingdom, President John F. Kennedy made America popular for its democracy, religious tolerance, freedom of speech, and opportunity for self-actualization.

Despite more than five decades as a proud United States citizen and passionate Texan, I don't think there will ever be a time I will become desensitized from news coverage of gun violence. It is tragically unsurprising that— in a country where guns cause 40,000 deaths and 100,000 injuries annually— Americans possess more guns per capita than any other country.

In all my decades experience as a physician, before I retired in 2015, I pledged to be there for my patients however I could, to do everything in my power to improve and save lives. As a psychiatrist, I've seen firsthand the ghastly physical and emotional toll gun violence takes on my patients as well as their communities.

Unfortunately, our lawmakers and the general population share a great tolerance for this mayhem. I have read hundreds of articles written by well-respected journalists and professionals who repeatedly recommend monitoring gun control through background checks. Most countries of the world follow this basic principle of gun control, except the United States.

I did some research and concluded that Americans are *obsessed* with owning guns. Unless this changes, we cannot improve the existing high incidence of gun violence. I am confident that if people change their ideas about the possession of guns, lawmakers will support stringent background checks.

MASS SHOOTINGS IN THE UNITED STATES

The United States has the highest incident of gun violence per capita in the world. According to the Gun Violence Archive[i] in 2021, more than one mass shooting per day has occurred.

It's fair to say that we in the United States have beaten a grim world record. According to Wikipedia, there were over 637 mass shootings in United States in 2021 alone. The survivors of those horrific tragedies pleaded for change, but no one listened.

After resigning from his job, a worker was able to walk into a building and kill twelve people in Virginia Beach on May 31, 2019. On August 3, 2019, a 21-year-old man killed twenty-two people and wounded more than two dozen at an El Paso, Texas, shopping center. One day later, in Dayton, Ohio, police officers killed a shooter within 32 seconds of his opening fire, but he still managed to kill nine people in those few seconds with an assault weapon. A few weeks later in

---

i   Gun Violence Archive, accessed November 24, 2021, https://www.gunviolencearchive.org/.

Odessa, Texas, a man killed seven and wounded many more. Earlier, in the last week of July, a shooter killed three people and wounded thirteen others at a garlic festival in Gilroy, California. According to FBI this is a phenomenon which is the greatest terrorist threat to America.[1]

During this same period, a man fatally shot two people in Santa Maria, California, over an argument about golf and then went on to kill two more people in a nearby mobile home. A man in San Jose killed four members of his wife's family while they were having dinner. A teenager in Alabama was accused of killing five relatives; a father in Iowa killed his wife and two school-aged sons; a man in Oklahoma was charged with killing his wife and stepchildren; a triple homicide in rural Pennsylvania followed by suicide was perpetrated by a man suffering from post-traumatic stress disorder who had been fired from his job. Many children were killed in those shootings—in their homes, at a shopping center, on a highway, or in a park. Very few people heard about them, except through local media. None of them made it into national headlines because they didn't occur in public places.

Early in the 2020 pandemic, when people were concentrating on social distancing, wearing masks, and buying toilet paper due to predicted short supply, people bought two million guns because they were scared of a gun shortage.[2]

There are different motivations in mass shootings—bigotry, domestic arguments, simple anger, or road rage, to name a few. Sometimes, the reason for a massacre is never discovered, as in the case of one of the deadliest mass shootings in U.S. history which took place in Las Vegas. In the summer of 2019, more than half of the mass killing suspects had a familial or close relationship to at least one of their victims.

Research has shown that many mass shooters have a history of hating women, assaulting their wives, girlfriends, and other female family members, or sharing misogynistic views online. What is common to all of them is that whenever someone wants to kill, a gun can be found to do it. It is not simply anger or any other motivation that is the problem. Rather, it is the easy availability of guns which kill people.

Reports of hate crimes have been increasing for the past several years. A white racist killer with an AK-47 drove from Dallas, Texas, to El Paso, a U.S. border town, to kill Hispanics at a Walmart center. According to police, he appeared to have posted a racist, anti-immigrant manifesto online minutes before the attack, declaring the need for fighting the "Hispanic invasion of Texas." Just prior to the attack, Governor Greg Abbott had signed ten pro-gun bills into law, making it easier for Texans to buy military style arsenals for self-defense, like a soldier fighting in a hostile country.

Mass shootings make up only a small fraction of America's gun deaths, less than 2% in 2016. Yet 31% of the total number of global mass shooters come from the United States. Though the United States constitutes less than 5% of the world's population, Americans own 45% of all the world's privately held firearms.

After each mass shooting, we saw an outburst of articles published in major newspapers across the country, condemning the atrocities and calling for strong regulations on gun sales. Democrats promised to introduce bills on gun control. President Trump declared that "our nation must condemn racism and white supremacy; these sinister ideologies must be defeated," and claimed to be "…looking at a lot of different bills, ideas, concepts," though nothing came to fruition. As journalist Jonathan Capehart pointed out, nothing can happen "as long as the president of the United States is [the] chief promoter."[3]

Marianne Williamson, author, spiritual leader, and 2020 presidential candidate, claimed that Americans are not violent people; rather, America has a violent culture. She said that "our environmental policies are violent toward the Earth. Our criminal justice system is violent toward people of color. Our economic system is violent toward the poor. Our entertainment media is violent toward women. Our video games are violent in their effect on the minds of children. Our military is violent in ways and places where it doesn't have to be. And our government is indirectly and directly violent in the countless ways it uses its power to help those who do not need help and to withhold support from those who do."[4]

I agree with Ms. Williamson's analysis. Her observations support the long-term goal to change American culture, but I believe we don't have time to wait. We need to take immediate action to educate people about the dangers of gun possession, restrict gun sales, and root out people who should not own guns under any circumstances.

After each mass shooting, newspapers published articles demanding gun control legislation; Democrats promised to introduce bills for gun regulations; and the president and Republicans, as usual, sent thoughts and prayers to the families of victims, blaming mental health as the cause of atrocities, but doing nothing to control gun violence.

The number of people killed in mass shootings is relatively negligible compared to the 40,000 annual deaths in the United States due to gun violence. The problem of gun violence and the resulting tragedies is more complex and requires a thorough evaluation. Therefore, I wrote this article to present all aspects of this complex issue.

For the last two decades, many articles have been written about the rising gun violence in America. Several recommendations have been made to control or reduce the death and destruction caused by gun violence. Most of these articles focused on the absence of control on gun sales and the NRA's influence on legislators to oppose the restriction of laws controlling the purchase of guns. Some articles emphasized the importance of the second amendment and the right of every individual to own a gun to defend themselves.

Two opposing views are presented: one group suggests more restrictions on the sales of guns so that less guns are available, which will reduce suicide, homicide, accidental deaths, and mass shootings. The other group supports the birth right of Americans to own guns for self-defense with minimal restrictions.

WHY DO AMERICANS HAVE AN OBSESSION ABOUT POSSESSING GUNS?

After reviewing several of articles, I concluded that Americans love guns and want to own guns. If most Americans want to control gun sales, they would have pressured legislators for strict background checks and the prohibition of the sale of guns capable of mass destruction.

Americans make up 4% of the world's population but own about 46% of the entire global stock of the 857 million civilian firearms. There are more than 400 million civilian-owned firearms in the United States, or enough for every man, woman, and child to own one and still have 67 million guns left over.[5]

With an estimated 120.5 guns for every one hundred residents, the firearm ownership rate in the United States is the highest in the world. France and Germany have a rate of 19.6 guns per one hundred residents whereas in the United Kingdom there are 4.9 guns per one hundred residents. In the United States, 36.3% of people have access to a gun and 5%

carry a gun with them. A strong relationship emerges between gun ownership and homicide.[6]

Americans are obsessed with possessing guns. Is it due to a genetic inheritance or acquired behavior? To formulate an opinion, I started looking at the history of settlements in America since the beginning of the 17th century, when the first settlers arrived in May 1607. When you look in detail at history, one sees that those early settlers in the east and the adventurers who moved west in the 17th to 19th centuries, faced extreme hardship. The first settlers did not have enough food or fresh water and suffered from severe disease without available healthcare. In addition, there was no law and order. Leadership was inadequate and governance weak. Fifty to sixty percent of early settlers died due to starvation and diseases. The *National Geographic* stated that starvation in early settlers resulted in cannibalism.[7]

On top of that, the most serious problem that settlers faced was conflict with indigenous people, hoodlums in the community, and protection from the wildlife. Since there was a lack of law and order and settlers lived in lawless communities, it became necessary to have weapons for their self-protection.

Lacking regular law enforcement, settlers often resorted to justice by self-appointed citizen groups. I do not want to go into detail about the horrors the early settlers faced in the new world to have a better life. However, for over three hundred years, settlers and adventurers had to rely on guns for self-defense (Western movies give us an idea about life in the 18th and 19th centuries and the use of guns.) These facts made it clear to me that what people for four to six generations learned living in America became so deeply engrained that now people are born with the innate feeling that they must have a gun to protect themselves.

It is hard to believe that in the 21st century people in the United States are still obsessed with owning the gun for self-protection and organizing "peace police" and "peace militia" as they did in the 16th century.

In Pennsylvania, a church, the World Peace and Unification Sanctuary, held a ceremony attended by hundreds of couples clutching AR-15s while they renewed their wedding vows. The church encouraged couples to bring the weapons because the AR-15 is a symbol of the "rod of iron" referenced in the biblical book of Revelation. While protesters gathered outside to condemn the ceremony, Reverend Sean Moon called on worshippers to pray for "a kingdom of peace police and peace militia" in which citizens can protect each other through the right to bear arms "given to them by almighty God." Worshippers who attended the ceremony saw it as a way to double-down on defending the Second Amendment. One attendee, Sreymom Ouk, told the Associated Press that her AR-15 represented her right to defend against "sickos and evil psychopaths."[8]

The church ceremony in Pennsylvania is a clear example of obsessive behavior to possess guns for self-protection, something which would never occur in economically well-to-do countries of the world. Is the obsession to own a gun genetically determined behavior or is it an acquired behavior? I leave it to scientists to do in-depth research and draw a conclusion.

Before I discuss in detail the current situation related to gun violence, it is important to understand why people have such a preoccupation with the possession of guns. In 21st century America, one of the most civilized countries in the world, there is excellent law and order and no fear of wildlife; therefore, we do not need guns to protect ourselves and our families. No logical reason exists for claiming that everyone needs a gun for self-protection. Self-protection from what? Obsession with owning guns is an acquired or genetically determined behavior, which has been going on for six generations.

Democrats say that 90% of Americans support universal background checks. Yet, Republican lawmakers voted against expanded gun control measures. More Americans say that they lean more towards the Republican party than the Democratic party on gun policy.[9] Most Americans want to own guns, with the least restrictions. Pew's latest poll on the subject show that 79% of Republicans favor protecting gun ownership rights over limiting gun access and 20% of Democrats felt the same way.[10] Most Democrats are of diverse ethnicity. Their ancestors may be latecomers, descendants of African Americans, or people from other parts of the world who arrived in the nineteenth or twentieth centuries. They strongly support more restrictions on gun ownership.

    I authored this article for people who strongly believe that owning a gun is every American's birthright and who minimize the grave consequences of the availability of stockpiles of guns and the resulting loss and suffering of millions of people.

GUN VIOLENCE IS AN EPIDEMIC

Americans are twenty-five times more likely to be murdered with a gun than people in other developed countries. According to national statistics, over 40,000 deaths per year are caused by guns. Over 22,000 people commit suicide, and homicide takes another 13,000 lives. About five hundred people are accidently killed by guns, and another five hundred are killed by police. It is estimated that over 100,000 people are injured each year by gunshots, either by attempted homicide, attempted suicide, or accidents.[11]

The suicide rate by guns is ten times that of other high-income countries. Five percent of all suicide attempts result in death, while 85% of suicide attempts by guns end in death.[12,13,14]

The level of gun violence in the United States is one of the highest in the world, with 4.43 deaths per 100,000 people. That is nine times the rate in Canada, which has 0.47 deaths per 100,000 people. In Singapore it's 0.02; Japan, 0.04; Indonesia, 0.04; Oman, 0.04; China, 0.04; South Korea, 0.05; United Kingdom, 0.06; Iceland, 0.07; Bangladesh, 0.07; and Romania 0.08.

In those countries where gun violence is substantially higher than that of the United States—in particular in Central and South America and the Caribbean—it is due to the presence of gangs related to drug trafficking, as in Salvador, Venezuela, Jamaica, Columbia, and Brazil. Even Middle Eastern countries infested with sectarian violence, such as Afghanistan, Lebanon, Pakistan, Syria, Iraq, and Libya, have less incidence of death by gun violence than the United States. The United States is one of only three countries, along with Mexico and Guatemala, which assumes people have an inherent right to own guns.[15]

Of the world's annual 251,000-gun deaths, more than half of them occur in six countries—Brazil, Mexico, Columbia, Venezuela, Guatemala, and the United States. Except for the U.S., those countries have weak economies and a weak judicial system. The United States was one of seventeen countries in which both the firearm homicide rate and the firearm suicide rate are higher than the global median.

We often hear about death and injuries, but we seldom discuss the devastating effect on survivors. The psychological and financial consequence on survivors is hard to believe. A few years ago, a man killed his wife with a gun in a family dispute. He was arrested and received a life sentence. The surviving five children aged two to ten were placed in different foster homes. After five years, no one has come forward to adopt them. They must live with the scars of severe psychological trauma for the rest of their lives. The damage is unmeasurable. Psychological trauma can happen from natural causes, but more frequently it is due to gun violence. The husband had a history of domestic abuse, but he was still able to purchase a gun.

Since the shooting at Columbine High, almost 200,000 students have been exposed to gun violence in schools and experienced profound trauma following mass shootings in the school. Their emotional and psychological wounds are often unrecognized. Understanding and treating each person's unique suffering takes time and is expensive. There are not enough counsellors to provide supportive counselling services. No one has studied the long-term psychological effects on these young people. Most of them experience anger, guilt, and depression. Two former students at Stoneman Douglas High School in Parkland, Florida, took their own life in 2019, after struggling with survivor's guilt and post-traumatic stress disorder.[16]

A major reason for the United States' high death rate from guns is due to gun ownership and the weak laws governing it. The United States does not have more crime than other developed countries, but it does have more lethal violence due to the access to guns. People everywhere get into arguments and have fights with friends, family, and peers. But in the United States, it is much more likely that someone will be able to pull out a gun and kill another. America has some of the weakest gun laws in the developed world, effectively allowing civilians to own firearms at much greater levels than anywhere else. Until the United States confronts this issue, it will continue to see more gun deaths than in the rest of the developed world.[17]

In the United States, we are accustomed to hearing about shootings. We have become desensitized and accept it as normal. A Michigan man fatally shot his wife after mistaking her for an intruder. He and his two children aged two and four must live with that trauma for the rest of their lives. In another incident on the July 4th weekend in 2019, a young Texan man filled with road rage got out of his car and fired at a truck that was carrying fireworks, resulting in a blast that critically burned two young children. On November 14 of the same year, a 16-year-old high school student pulled a gun from his backpack in Santa Clarita, California, and killed two and injured five students in 16 seconds.

On November 21, a Los Angeles student was arrested after he allegedly threatened to shoot classmates and staff at his school. A search led to the seizure of an AR-15 rifle and a large amount of ammunition that he purchased through the internet. What kind of damage could he have inflicted? Our kids are living in fear, not knowing when and where a shooting will happen next.

After a mass shooting in Britain in 1987, the country instituted strict gun control laws. Australia did the same. After a man killed thirty-five people with a semi-automatic weapon in Port Arthur, Tasmania in 1996, the country implemented sweeping gun control measures. Then-Prime Minister John Howard could not have made it any clearer, "Australia will not be like the United States." Australia has not had a fatal mass shooting since.

Australia's experience demonstrates that banning rapid-fire firearms is associated with reductions in mass shootings and firearm deaths. The United States repeatedly faces the same situation but decides that unregulated gun ownership is worth the cost to society. A British journalist wrote in a 2012 post, "Once America decided killing children was bearable, the debate over gun control was over."[18]

After a mass shooting at two New Zealand mosques, well-respected *New York Times* columnist Nicholas Kristof summarized well the cultural differences and its impact on gun laws. When a terrorist massacred fifty people at two New Zealand mosques, Prime Minister Jacinda Ardern immediately grasped the situation. "I can tell you one thing right now," she told a news conference, "our gun laws will change." Contrast that with the United States, where, since 1970, more Americans have died from guns (1.45 million, including murders, suicides, and accidents) than died in all the wars in American history (1.4 million). More Americans die from guns in ten weeks (January to March 2019) than died in the entire Afghanistan and Iraqi wars combined, yet we still don't have gun safety rules as rigorous as New Zealand's even before the mosques were attacked.

The argument is that the killer's hate, not his guns and bullets, were the real problem. Without weapons of mass murder, fifty New Zealand worshipers would still be alive; seventeen Parkland, Florida, schoolchildren, and staff members would still be alive; nine Charleston, South Carolina, churchgoers would still be alive; eleven Pittsburgh congregants would still be alive; fifty-eight Las Vegas concertgoers would still be alive; twenty-six Newtown, Connecticut, first-graders and adults would still be alive. Every day in America, another hundred people die from gun violence and three hundred more are injured. Yet, our president and Congress do nothing.[19]

When there is a demand for guns, it is easier for gun lobbyists to raise capital from gun manufacturers to promote the sales of guns. In a capitalist society, the primary goal is to make a profit even at the cost of human lives. In the 1950s, we learned about the relationship between tobacco use and lung cancer. Even so, it took many years and thousands of lives before the government finally passed laws to stop the advertisement of tobacco, raised the age for purchasing cigarettes, and educated people about tobacco use and cancer. People who were addicted didn't want restrictions on tobacco sales; ethical and moral concerns took a back seat.

Gun violence is the most outrageous epidemic in the history of this country. Many people do not feel safe and secure in their schools, workplaces, places of worship, shopping malls, places of entertainment, or even on the street. Unfortunately, the NRA, members of Congress who are heavily funded by the NRA, and even our presidents are not influenced by the suffering caused by gun violence.

President Trump wanted to put more guns on the street by placing no restrictions on gun purchases, arming teachers, removing any remaining restrictions on the purchase of silencers, and supporting concealed carry weapons. Even in response to the tragedies in Virginia, Las Vegas, Orlando, Sandy Hook, Colorado, and most recently in El Paso, Dayton, and Odessa, Texas, Congress did not act to make our communities safer. This is a pathetic example of giving priority to corporate financial gains over the loss of human lives.

Many articles written in the last two decades focus on the high incidence of gun violence, the absence of control over gun sales. and the NRA's influence on legislators. Other articles emphasize the importance of the Second Amendment and the right of every individual to own a gun for self-defense. Some promote more restrictions on gun sales to reduce the number of available guns and the rates of suicide, homicide, accidental deaths, and mass shootings. Still others support Americans' birthright to own guns for self-defense; they claim more guns will make America safer. Given that we already have the highest number of gun sales in the world, we should already be the safest place on earth and have less crime, but that's far from the case. The problem of gun violence and its concomitant tragedies is far more complex and requires a more thorough evaluation.

MENTAL ILLNESS SUICIDE AND DEATH BY GUN VIOLENCE

I am a psychiatrist who has been treating patients with mental illness for over fifty years. It is believed that if a man killed dozens of people, he could be regarded as mentally deranged. Likewise, we frequently hear President Trump, Republican legislators, or NRA officials dismiss a mass shooter by claiming that he or she had mental problems. Therefore, the perpetrator of the heinous crime of a mass shooting is often said to have mental health issues. It is a way to deflect attention away from other more difficult issues, such as racism, terrorism, and the lack of gun control.

Media coverage of mass shootings by disturbed individuals catches the public's attention and reinforces the popular belief that mental illness often results in violence. Epidemiological studies show that most people with serious mental illnesses are seldom violent. If a person's mental health[ii]

---

ii Benedict Carey, "Are Mass Murderers Insane? Usually Not, Researchers Say," *The New York Times*, November 9, 2017, https://www.nytimes.com/2017/11/08/health/mass-murderers-mental-illness.html.

made such a significant difference, then data would show that Americans have more mental health[iii] problems than people in other countries. But Americans do not have more mental health problems than those in other economically developed countries.

One of the largest studies of mass killers, conducted by Dr. Michael Stone and involving 350 people, found that only 20% had a psychotic illness; the other 80% had no diagnosable mental illness, only the everyday stress, anger, jealousy, and unhappiness the rest of us have. Ordinary human hatred and aggression are far more dangerous than any psychiatric illness.[20]

Brendon Tarrant, who murdered fifty-one people last March in a mosque in Christchurch, New Zealand, was found at trial not to be mentally ill. Rather, he was a white supremacist who planned his terrorist attack for two years. And like Mr. Crusius, he believed in a white supremacist conspiracy theory known as "the great replacement," which posits that white Europeans, with the complicity of "elites," are being replaced by non-European people through mass immigration.[21]

As Jeffrey Swanson summarized so well about suicide, mental illness is most often the reason people try to end their own lives, and access to a firearm used to die by suicide is most often the reason they do not survive.[22]

Isaac Bailey wrote, "Predicting human behavior is among the most difficult things to do. Predicting who will commit violence before the violence is committed is even more difficult."[23]

Binder and Hirschtritt summarized several studies that suggest serious mental illness is not a specific indicator for the risk of violence. The article notes that studies have found

---

iii   Max Fisher and Josh Keller, "Why Does the U.S. Have so Many Mass Shootings? Research Is Clear: Guns.," *The New York Times,* November 7, 2017, https://www.nytimes.com/2017/11/07/world/americas/mass-shootings-us-international.html.

that people with mental illness are three times more likely to be victims than perpetrators of violence, and only 4% of criminal violence in the United States can be attributed to people with mental illness. Most people with mental illness will never commit a mass shooting; instead, this rhetoric leads to increased shame, societal rejection, and stigmatization.[24,25]

Federal law prohibits anyone committed to a mental health facility or deemed dangerous or lacking all mental capacities from owning a gun. Reporting mental health data to the National Instant Criminal Background Check System may reduce violent crimes committed by people with mental illness. Family members of patients with mental illness can get court orders to disarm relatives who might do harm to themselves.

However, mental illness is strongly associated with increased risk of suicide, which accounts for over half of U.S. firearms-related fatalities in the United States each year. Gun homicides get far more attention in the media, but empirical studies prove that most gun deaths are the result of suicide not homicide. In 2016, according to the Center for Disease Control (CDC), 22,938 people committed suicide by firearm, while 14,415 people died from gun homicides.

Improving mental health treatment will help many people. Yet, the United States has the highest rate of gun deaths not because Americans have higher rates of mental illness than the rest of the world, but because it's so easy for people to own a deadly weapon. If mental health[iv] made a difference, the data would show that Americans have more mental health[v] problems than do people in other countries with fewer mass shootings. However, spending on mental health care in the United States, the number of mental health professionals per

---

iv See note ii.
v See note iii.

capita, and the rate of severe mental health[vi] are all in line with those of other economically developed countries.[26]

According to the CDC an individual is at a higher risk of attempting or committing suicide when they're dealing with alcohol and opioid addiction, relationship issues, or health problems. Serious emotional trauma and stress, such as divorce, job loss, and social media's cyberbullying have been identified as key factors increasing one's risk for engaging in suicide.

In every age group, firearms were the leading mechanism for suicide deaths. Access to a firearm, particularly during a time of stress, increased risk of suicide. Several studies have shown that rates of suicide are higher in states with higher levels of gun ownership and that these heightened rates are driven by increases in firearm suicides.

While suicide is a subject familiar to Americans, guns as a vehicle for suicide are not. A common assumption is that suicide is premeditated, giving a person ample time to obtain access to a highly lethal means such as a firearm. However, while some suicides are planned, many suicide attempts occur within less than an hour of thinking about them; a person experiencing an acutely distressing incident may respond impulsively to suicidal thoughts.[27]

The United States has the highest rate of firearm suicides of all twenty-seven developed nations, whereas the United States has the 16th highest rate of suicide overall. Children in the United States have ten times the gun suicide rate as kids in France and Australia and other developed countries.

Suicide attempts involving a firearm are more likely to result in death than attempts using any other means. If firearms are available to a person who is thinking about taking his or

---

vi   Ronald C. Kessler et al., "The Global Burden of Mental Disorders: An Update from The Who World Mental Health (WMH) Surveys," *Epidemiologia e Psichiatria Sociale* 18, no. 1 (2009): pp. 23-33, https://doi.org/10.1017/s1121189x00001421.

her life, the presence of firearms may be linked with a higher likelihood of suicide. In homes with firearms, 86% of the individuals who committed suicide used a firearm. In homes without firearms, only 6% of the individuals who committed suicide used a firearm.[28]

Recent studies from the Boston University School of Public Health found that youth suicide rates are higher in states with high gun ownership rates. For each ten-percentage-point increase in household gun ownership, the youth suicide rate increased by 26.9%. The four states with the highest youth suicide rates—Alaska, South Dakota, Wyoming, and Montana—also have the highest rates of firearm ownership. Likewise, four states with the lowest rates of youth suicide—New York, New Jersey, Massachusetts, and Rhode Island—are in the bottom four for levels of gun ownership. A study by the Harvard School of Public Health of all fifty U.S. states also reveals a powerful link between rates of firearm ownership and suicides. These studies demonstrate that the strongest single predictor of a state's youth suicide rate is the prevalence of household gun ownership in that state.[29, 30]

Suicide by a firearm is quick and immediately lethal; whereas suffocation, pills, or other methods take longer and are more likely to fail to kill. Most suicidal attempters act on impulse, in moments of panic or despair. Once the acute feelings ease, 90% do not go on to die by suicide. Many suicide attempts occur with little planning, often in response to a short-term crisis. Those who impulsively attempt suicide with a gun rarely get a chance to reconsider the decision. So, it is reasonable to suspect that if guns are less available, fewer suicide attempts with firearms will result in fatality, and more people will have the chance to reconsider their suicidal decisions.[31]

How can lives be saved?

As a psychiatrist who has considerable experience with suicidal patients, I fully agree with the American Public Health Association's recommendations that many lives would be saved if people disposed of their firearms, kept them locked away, or stored them outside the home beyond the reach of a potentially suicidal patient.

Ninety percent of people who attempted suicide and survived did not go on to die by suicide later. One is more likely to survive a suicide attempt if one does not use the most highly lethal means available to make that attempt. A recent CDC report noted that 54% of suicide decedents in twenty-seven states in 2015 did not have a known mental health condition prior to suicide.

The most promising evidence-based strategies to reduce access to firearms during a period of high risk are temporary relocation of household firearms away from the home or safe storage at home and increased screening for and counseling about access to guns by health professionals, law enforcement officers, and others.

Gun Ownership for Older Adults with Mental Disturbance and Dementia

More than 37% of senior adults in the United States report that they live in a home where guns are present. About 13% of Americans older than sixty-five have some degree of dementia. Several individuals with dementia who died by suicide or were responsible for a homicide used a firearm. The rate of suicide by firearm is highest among older adults.

During the early stages of dementia, there is an inability to comprehend that an impairment exists. People convince themselves that there is nothing wrong with their reasoning.

At the same time, they are aware of their cognitive dysfunction. This often leads to depression and suicidal ideas.

Some patients with dementia may confuse a caretaker with an intruder and shoot the individual. Unfortunately, many individuals live by themselves and have periodic visits from caretakers, unless they suffer from a serious medical problem. Since many Americans have weapons to protect their homes and families, the suggestion that guns be made inaccessible to an individual diagnosed with dementia is often met with resistance. If an individual is declared totally incompetent, it is easier to remove the gun.[32]

A 24 to 48-hour waiting time to purchase a firearm may prevent many suicides. Commonly if guns are not easily available at home, the suicidal individual may buy a gun from any gun shop. Since many suicidal individuals do not have a criminal record or history of serious mental illness, they can easily buy a gun unless a 24- to 48-hour restriction is imposed. In that case, it is hoped the individual may overcome their suicidal impulses.[27]

Domestic Violence

Fifty-two percent of American women killed with guns are murdered by partners or family members, and women in the United States are twenty-one times more likely to be killed with a gun than women in other developed countries.[33] Access to a gun in a situation of domestic violence makes it five times more likely that a woman will be killed.[34]

Federal law prohibits the purchase of a gun online without a background check by anyone who has a history of domestic violence. However, the law doesn't keep guns from abusers who are not married, do not live with their partner, or do not share a child with them. This is irrational as women are also killed by boyfriends. In fact, more than one million women have been shot by an intimate partner.[35]

GUN VIOLENCE IS KILLING MORE CHILDREN

Two million minors in the United States live in homes where firearms are loaded and easy to access. Firearms are the second leading cause of death for American children and teens. Nearly 1,700 children and teens die by gun homicide every year. As many as 107,391 children are rushed to the hospital every year because of gun injuries from accidents at home.[36] An estimated 54% of the gun owners keep their guns unsecured.[37]

The Centers for Disease Control and Prevention reported that the rate of gun deaths of children 14 and younger rose by roughly 50 percent from the end of 2019 to the end of 2020. The number of children and teenagers killed by gunfire has risen sharply during the coronavirus pandemic due to a surge of pandemic gun-buying.[vii] According to the CDC, guns accounted for 14,000 child deaths over a period of ten years and are the second leading cause of deaths of children in the

---

vii https://www.nytimes.com/2022/01/05/us/american-children-gun- deaths.html

United States.[38] Yet, the NRA opposes gun storage laws and gun education.[39]

Sixty-five percent of unintentional child gun deaths occur in homes where guns were irresponsibly stored. Millions of U.S. children are placed at a higher risk of fatal firearm injuries and suicidal or accidental deaths because 40% of households with children contain firearms.

Many children are killed accidentally due to parental negligence. A Wisconsin man was arrested in January of 2022 after a gun he was handling discharged and killed an 8-year-old girl.[viii] In the same month, an 8-year-old girl named Melissa was walking with her mother in their Chicago neighborhood when she was struck by stray bullets after an unknown offender shot multiple times in their direction. A 6-month-old baby was killed in a drive-by shooting in Atlanta. Police say the rise in chaotic gunplay between rivals, or drive-by shootings, is especially risky for children in dangerous neighborhoods but it should not happen to any child anywhere[ix].

Kids play with guns as they think that they were playing with the toys. A 5-year-old was fatally shot after a 3-year-old cousin found a gun under a sofa cushion. 3-year-old boy was wounded after he found a gun under a bed and shot himself in the stomach. A 14-year-old boy shot and killed his 2-year brother while playing with the gun. In the Houston area, a four-year-old shot himself in the head and a 15-year-old was accidently shot by his brother.

The safest home for a child is one without firearms.[40] Alarmingly, one study found that of the teens with guns in their home who had attempted suicide in the past year, 40% had easy access to the firearm. Another study from the

---

viii   ixhttps://www.yahoo.com/news/wisconsin-man-handling-firearm-discharged-172350595.html
ix   https://www.npr.org/2022/01/28/1076396871/gun-violence-rise-killing-children-pandemic

federal government shows that 68% of school shootings are perpetrated by shooters who obtain a gun from their home or the home of relatives.[41]

THE SECOND AMENDMENT AND INDIVIDUALS' RIGHT TO BEAR ARMS

Sarah Sanders, the former White House press secretary, once said, "We have guns because it's our God-given right enshrined in the Constitution."

Whenever the topic of gun violence and gun control arises, people often refer to the Second Amendment. People like to claim that their right to possess a deadly weapon is so important that it is protected by the Constitution. Late Supreme Court Justice John Paul Stevenson clarified this distorted perception when he wrote:

> *Soon after Independence, Americans were concerned about the potential of excessive influence from the newly formed federal government and created the first ten amendments to place limits on its powers. Concern for the threat a national standing army could pose to the security of individual states led to the adoption of the Second Amendment. Hence, the wording of the amendment: a well-regulated Militia, being necessary*

to the security of a free State, the right of the people to keep and bear Arms, shall not be infringed. It should be noted that people were also protecting themselves from lawlessness, hostile tribes, and wildlife at that time.[42]

For more than two hundred years following the adoption of the Second Amendment, federal judges uniformly understood that the right to protection by the amendment was limited in two ways. First, it applied only to keeping and bearing arms for military purposes, Secondly, while it limited the power of the federal government, it did not impose any limit whatsoever on the power of states or local governments to regulate the use of firearms.

The amendment itself points to the need for a "well-regulated militia," suggesting that the right to own and use a gun is subordinate to the need for collective self-defense. Today, each state maintains a national guard and the federal government does not impose any restrictions on them. Therefore, there is no need for individuals to own arms to protect the state.

Given that the United States is one of the most civilized countries in the world and that every state and municipality has a police department to protect the lives of its citizens, we should repeal or revise the Second Amendment. Alternatively, we should revise the amendment to define the relationship between public safety and the rights of people to own guns. It could give clear safeguards for people with no history of legal trouble or mental instability to continue to own guns while giving more authority to the government to guarantee that only people unlikely to misuse guns would have them.

The NRA disagrees with this position and has mounted a vigorous campaign claiming that federal regulation of the use of firearms severely curtails Second Amendment rights. According to retired Chief Justice Burger, the Second

Amendment "has been the subject of one of the greatest pieces of fraud on the American public by special interest groups that I have ever seen in my lifetime."

In all other developed countries, semiautomatic assault weapons and ammunition magazines are banned. Machine guns and similar weapons of mass destruction may be useful in war, but these weapons should not be protected by the Second Amendment, which protects the use of weapons for lawful purposes only, such as self-defense. Too many people die needlessly because of gun laws that do not prevent unstable people from possessing weapons of mass murder.

In 2008, the Supreme Court clearly supported the individual's right to keep a gun at home[x] for self-defense. But for the seventy years or so prior, the U.S. Supreme Court and federal courts held that the Second Amendment pertained only in the context of militias, i.e., the right of states to protect themselves from federal interference.

When the Supreme Court decided the District of Columbia versus Heller case five to four, overturning a handgun ban in the city, conservative Justice Antonin Scalia wrote the opinion in narrow but unprecedented terms. For the first time in the country's history, the Supreme Court explicitly affirmed an individual's right to keep a weapon at home for self-defense. Justice Scalia wrote several exceptions, such as bans on "dangerous and unusual weapons" and no sales to domestic abusers and people with mental illness. He also wrote that states and cities could ban firearms from places like government buildings. Justice John Paul Stevens dissented, saying the decision showed disrespect "for the well-settled

---

[x] Alan Yuhas, "The Right to Bear Arms: What Does the Second Amendment Really Mean?," *The Guardian*, October 5, 2017, https://www.theguardian.com/us-news/2017/oct/05/second-amendment-right-to-bear-arms-meaning-history.

views of all of our predecessors on the court, and for the rule of law itself." [xi]

Carl Bogus, a law professor at Roger Williams University, has argued that James Madison wrote the Second Amendment in part to reassure his home state of Virginia, where slave owners were terrified of revolts and wary of Northerners who would undermine the system. After the Civil War, Second Amendment rights were again debated by Congress, which abolished militias[xii] in the former Confederate states and passed the 1866 Civil Rights Act,[xiii] explicitly protecting freed slaves' right[xiv] to bear arms. The state's conservative lawmakers promptly took up the cause of gun control. In 1967, Governor Ronald Reagan signed the Mulford Act, banning the public carry of loaded guns in cities. Reagan said he saw[xv] no reason why on streets today a citizen should be carrying loaded weapons.[43]

In 2018, late Justice Stevens asked for a repeal of the Second Amendment. "A constitutional amendment to get rid of the Second Amendment would be simple and would do more to weaken the NRA's ability to stymie legislative debate and block constructive gun control legislation than any other available option."[44]

---

xi District of Columbia et al. v. Heller, No. 07–290. Argued March 18, 2008—Decided June 26, 2008, Supreme Court of the United States, https://www.supremecourt.gov/opinions/07pdf/07-290.pdf

xii John Massaro, *No Guarantee of a Gun: How and Why the Second Amendment Means Exactly What It Says*, 614, Bloomington, IN: Authorhouse, 2009.

xiii Michael Stokes Paulsen et al., *The Constitution of the United States* (St. Paul, MN: Foundation Press, 2013).

xiv Ezra Klein, "A History of the Second Amendment in Two Paintings," *The Washington Post* (WP Company, April 28, 2019), https://www.washingtonpost.com/news/wonk/wp/2012/12/15/a-history-of-the-second-amendment-in-two-paintings/.

xv Peter Laufer, *The Elusive State of Jefferson: A Journey through the 51st State* (Guilford, CT: TwoDot, an imprint of Globe Pequot Press, 2013).

Second Amendment Preservation Act[xvi]

Recently many state legislatures have passed or attempting to pass this amendment. It represents a challenge to federal authority and all state firearms laws that "exceed" the federal government's power to track, register, and regulate guns and gun owners. The law features a provision that allows Missourians to sue local law departments that give "material aid and support" to federal agents—defined as data sharing, joint operations, even social media posts—in violation of citizens' perceived Second Amendment rights. The provision allows citizens to sue any local police agency for $50,000 for every incident in which they can prove that their rights were violated, thus making some local officials afraid to collaborate with federal partners. Even on routine criminal cases, at a time when greater cooperation is needed, twelve of fifty-three officers withdrew from joint task force collaborations. State and local agencies have also begun to restrict federal access to investigative resources, including the Missouri Information Analysis Center, a state crime database, and the Kansas City Police Department's records system.

The law has caused significant harm as it decreased public safety by stigmatizing all interactions between local federal agents and related gun violence.[45]

---

xvi "Governor Parson Signs HB 85 Establishing Second Amendment Preservation Act," June 14, 2021, https://governor.mo.gov/press-releases/archive/governor-parson-signs-hb-85-establishing-second-amendment-preservation-act.

CONGRESS INHIBITS RESEARCH PROPOSALS RELATED TO CAUSES AND EFFECTS OF FIREARM VIOLENCE

There is no law or set of laws that can completely prevent every senseless act of violence. However, it is our moral and ethical responsibility to do whatever we can to reduce this human tragedy. We must do everything we can to free the Bureau of Alcohol, Tobacco, Firearms and Explosives (ATF) and other federal agencies to use their knowledge and expertise to protect our communities from future gun-related tragedies.

We need to remove restrictions contained within policy riders on ATF's activities, which are tightly controlled by Congress. The ATF has been prohibited from creating a centralized database of gun sales records even though it is the licensing body for firearms dealers and is responsible for ensuring that federally licensed firearms dealers comply with the laws and regulations that govern their businesses. Irresponsible gun dealers create an opportunity for guns to be diverted to dangerous individuals and criminal gun-trafficking networks.

The Tiahrt Trace Data Amendment barred the ATF from disclosing any trace data to the public. The FBI can only retain records of individuals who successfully passed the National Instant Criminal Background Check System. This compromises law enforcement's ability to identify straw purchasers—a person who buys a gun for someone who can't legally purchase a gun—and purchases by criminal gun-trafficking networks. The NRA argues that requiring licensed gun dealers to maintain an inventory would be unduly burdensome on law-abiding dealers. No organization has done more to inhibit the law-enforcement functions of the ATF and other federal agencies than the NRA.[46]

Why do Americans use firearms to murder each other twenty times as often as people in other developed nations? What is triggering the violent impulses in so many troubled young people? Would more guns make us safer, or would they merely increase our risk? How do so many dangerous people slip through the cracks in our laws, and can anything be done to stop them? Why has the United States far exceeded death by gun violence than any other country in the world? The NRA does not want any finding that would affect the lucrative business of selling guns, even though it causes the death of hundreds of thousands of people, including young children. In Washington state and in state capitols across the country, the gun lobby has helped pass laws that restrict the collection and sharing of information related to guns and gun violence.

There were 307 mass shootings in the United States[xvii] in 2018. Every time people go to a mall, place of worship, movie theater, football game, concert, school, college, or even

---

xvii "Mass Shootings in 2021," Gun Violence Archive, accessed November 24, 2021, https://www.gunviolencearchive.org/reports/mass-shooting?page=24&sort=desc&order=State.

workplace, they look out into the gathering and wonder if there is a man with a gun in the crowd, pulling the trigger. Nobody is exempt or immune from facing this risk, including politicians and government officials, students from kindergarten through college, and innocent bystanders. A congressman was shot and critically wounded. Children at Sandy Hook Elementary were murdered. Revelers at the Pulse nightclub were murdered. People in a yoga studio and concertgoers in Las Vegas were murdered.

We need to know which interventions are most effective and how they can best be implemented to save the most lives. Congress refused funding for those proposals, and the Tiahrt amendments prevent the ATF from sharing its firearms-tracking database with anyone outside of law enforcement.[47]

The scarcity of research on firearm-related violence limits policy makers' ability to propose evidence-based policies to reduce injuries and deaths and maximize safety while recognizing Second Amendment rights. Since the 1960s, several state and federal laws and regulations have been enacted that restrict the government's ability to collect and share information about gun sales, ownership, and possession. Among them are the amendments to the Gun Control Act of 1968, which prohibits the federal government from establishing an electronic database with the names of gun purchasers and requires gun dealers to conduct annual inventories of their firearms.[48]

In addition to the restrictions on certain kinds of data collection, congressional action in 1996 effectively halted all firearm-related injury research at the CDC by prohibiting the use of federal funding "to advocate or promote gun control."[49]

In 2011, Congress enacted similar restrictions affecting the U.S. Department of Health and Human Services. As a result, the past twenty years have witnessed diminished progress in understanding the causes and effects of firearm violence.

High-quality data that is usable and accessible is fundamental to both the advancement of research and the development and evaluation of sound policies. Due to absence of relevant data, it is difficult to assess the prevalence, determine etiology, or effectively evaluate programs for potential reduction of harm and injury.

Policy makers need a wide array of information, including community-level data and data concerning the circumstances of firearm deaths, types of weapons used, victim–offender relationships, role of substance use, and geographic location of injury, none of which is consistently available.[50]

In 1993, the *New England Journal of Medicine* published a study by Arthur Kellerman, director of the RAND Institute of Health, that was funded by the Center for Disease Control (CDC). He found that firearm injuries were not random, unavoidable acts but were a preventable, public health issue. He stated that for every self-defense homicide by firearm, there were forty-three suicides, criminal homicides, or accidental gunshot deaths. He concluded that firearm ownership is a risk factor for both homicide and suicide in the home.

The study alarmed the NRA, which then aggressively pressured legislators to ban similar research because they were concerned about a decline in gun sales. The Dickey Amendment, a 1996 congressional appropriations bill, stipulated that "none of the funds made available for injury prevention and control at the CDC may be used to advocate or promote gun control."[51] Subsequently, Congress limited access to facts vital for understanding the gun violence pandemic in several ways.

Congress cut the CDC's budget by $2.6 million, which was the amount the agency had been spending on firearm research and passed the Dickey Amendment in 1996, with strong backing from the NRA. This amendment effectively bars the CDC from studying firearm violence. Specifically, no funds earmarked for injury prevention and control can be used to study the consequences of gun violence. CDC policy reinforces the government's prohibition on the use of CDC funds for research of gun issues "intended to restrict or control the purchase or use of firearms."

In 2003 Congress passed the Tiahrt Amendment, which significantly restricted law enforcement's ability to investigate gun crimes and prosecute unscrupulous gun dealers. The amendment prohibits the Bureau of Alcohol, Tobacco, Firearms and Explosives (ATF) from releasing firearm trace data for use by cities, states, researchers, litigants, and members of the public and requires the destruction of all approved gun purchaser records within 24 hours. This makes it extremely difficult for the ATF to retrieve firearms from persons prohibited from purchasing a gun. The destruction of gun purchaser records also limits the ATF's ability to trace gun-related crime and weakens law enforcement efforts to prevent crimes and prosecute gun offenders quickly and efficiently. The NRA argues that requiring licensed gun dealers to maintain an inventory of gun sales would be unduly burdensome on law-abiding dealers.

Gun dealer inventories facilitate enforcement of the federal law that requires dealers to report the loss or theft of firearms and helps law enforcement oversee the more than 50,000 firearms dealers nationwide. The results of these restrictions by Tiahrt Amendment have barred law enforcement agencies from accessing and sharing the data that could reveal patterns of gun trafficking or help identify gun dealers who sell guns illegally. Without firearm ownership records, it is difficult to remove firearms from persons convicted of a felony or who otherwise become ineligible for gun possession. In actuality, the Tiahrt Amendment protects unlawful gun dealers. Indeed, a 2012 study by researchers at Johns Hopkins Bloomberg School of Public Health found that the Tiahrt Amendment dramatically increased gun sales to criminals.

A 2016 study from the University of Pittsburgh Graduate School of Public Health found that in 2008, most guns recovered by police from crime scenes had been stolen.[xviii] Dr Richard Friedman, a renowned psychiatrist from New York City said, "We need to know which interventions are most effective and how they can best be implemented to save the most lives."

According to a 2008 analysis by the Brady Center, more than 30,000 guns in the inventories of firearms dealers were unaccounted for in 2007. The Tiahrt Amendment continues to prevent data disclosure to members of the public, including researchers and litigants, for use in lawsuits.

The repeal of the Dickey and Tiahrt amendments would enable Congress to base rational legislation on accurate information.

---

xviii https://www.sciencedaily.com/releases/2016/07/160725104118.htm

THE NRA AND LAWMAKERS

The NRA is a lobbying organization representing gun manufacturers and dealers who contribute millions of dollars to its support. They claim to be a grass-roots organization made of millions of decent, patriotic Americans who believe that guns in the hands of law-abiding citizens make our country safer. Unfortunately, the NRA is not concerned about the death of thousands of people due to easy access of guns and gives priority to selling guns with the least restrictions. Instead, the NRA tells the public that if they let research go forward, they will all lose their guns.

Corporate partners of the NRA have contributed millions of dollars to the organization. In turn, the NRA has spent millions of dollars on lobbying to protect the Dicky and Tiahrt laws by generously supporting the campaigns of legislators seeking re-election.[52,53]

In 2019, mass shootings killed twelve people in Virginia Beach. The Republican majority in Virginia, under the influence of the NRA, vigorously opposed a bill to strengthen gun laws through strict background checks and a ban on high-capacity magazines and silencers. They also opposed the bill for implementation of extreme-risk protective orders, which would have allowed law enforcement to temporarily remove firearms from individuals undergoing psychiatric treatment who pose a risk to themselves or to others. Virginia's Republicans chose to do nothing in face of a gun violence crisis that kills nearly one thousand Virginians every year. The lawmakers put the interests of the NRA ahead of public safety.[54]

It is to be noted that the Virginia Beach killer used a silencer as it was not outlawed. This prevented bystanders from running and calling 911 for help. For more than twenty years, Republicans and a few rural Democrats in the General Assembly have killed almost every measure aimed at restricting gun ownership. Additionally, the GOP blocked a major push for gun control after the 2007 Virginia Tech shootings, where thirty-three people died.[55]

Another example of how Republican lawmakers respond to any suggestion of gun control is the comment made by staunch NRA supporter Briscoe Cain of Texas. When Robert Francis "Beto" O'Rourke, a one-time presidential candidate, proposed a ban on certain military-style rifles shortly after the mass shooting in his hometown of El Paso in 2019 in which 22 people died and dozens were injured, Cain retorted by saying, "My AR is ready for you, Robert Francis."[xix]

Senator Marco Rubio from Florida, another Republican who strongly supports the NRA, proposed the implementation of red-flag laws, which would give law enforcement the ability to restrict access to guns for unstable and potentially violent people. It would certainly be a positive step to remove guns from people who have a history of violence. However, Rubio was careful not to use the words "background checks" in his proposed legislation. Even if his bill passes, it will not result in a significant reduction in gun deaths. Mr. Rubio is apologetic

---

xix Beto O'Rourke, accessed at https://www.theguardian.com/us-news/2019/sep/13/my-ar-15-is-ready-for-you-texas-lawmaker-tells-beto-orourke.

about sponsoring the bill and is quick to remind the public that the bill will not infringe on their right to own a gun and other Second Amendment rights of law-abiding gun owners.

Do firearms save lives?

Millions of Americans carry a firearm legally every day. Most people cite self-defense as the primary reason. Any discussion of firearms policy must acknowledge both the lives saved by the legal use of guns as well as the lives lost by criminal use.

The value of firearms in the hands of law-abiding citizens should be measured in terms of lives saved or crimes prevented. The exact number of Defending Gun Use (DGUs) is not precisely known. Many law-abiding people who successfully used a gun to deter a crime without firing a shot may choose not to report those incidents to the police. It is easy to measure the number of lives lost due to criminal gun violence. It is harder to measure the number of lives saved by legal defensive gun use.

In some incidents, there is no doubt that an intruder was scared off or killed by a gun in self-defense. However, one recent *Washington Post* story reported that, "For every criminal killed in self-defense, 34 innocent people died."[xx]

Is the purchase of a gun a birthright?

On Independence Day 2019, I read two articles with opposing points of view about Americans' right to own a gun to defend him or herself versus strict gun control to save thousands of lives. As a psychiatrist, I struggled for years with the logic and rationality of numerous issues discussed in the media. I eventually came to the conclusion that on any

---

xx   Christopher Ingraham "Guns in America: For every criminal killed in self-defense, 34 innocent people die" The Washington Post, June 19, 2015.

given issue, even the most intelligent arguments will elicit an opposing opinion. People come to different conclusions based on familial, cultural, social, religious. and emotional factors.

It is clear we have a problem with gun laws in this country. Justice Antonin Scalia wrote in his majority opinion in 2008's landmark Heller case, "Like most rights, the right secured by the Second Amendment is not unlimited." It is "not a right to keep and carry any weapon whatsoever in any manner whatsoever and for whatever purpose."[xxi] Contrary to this, with the blessings of NRA and support of legislatures, every American can purchase and carry guns with limited restrictions under the misinterpreted Second Amendment.

The NRA's stand on gun sales is based on the belief that every person has a birthright to own a gun. The NRA's motivation for making this assertion is purely economic. If one makes a lot of money selling guns, tobacco, or narcotics, one may not care about anything else, including risks to human beings and innocent children. One must wonder if, when twenty young children were gunned down in their classroom by a semiautomatic rifle in Newtown, Connecticut, did it not make a difference to the NRA?

Even entertaining for a moment that this was precisely the objective of the Second Amendment, American society has evolved. Rapid-fire weapons may prove effective in a war zone—but I cannot imagine the framers of the Constitution imagined civilians roaming about with machine guns during peacetime. Nonetheless, owning guns like these remains an obsession for countless Americans. Look no further than the 17-year-old accused of gunning down three people (killing two of them) at a Black Lives Matter demonstration in Kenosha one summer. The gun he was brandishing? A military-style, semi-automatic AR-15. The alleged shooter, authorities

---

[xxi] Justice Antonin Scalia, accessed at https://giffords.org/lawcenter/gun-laws/second-amendment/the-supreme-court-the-second-amendment.

said, traveled from his home in Northeast Illinois to the demonstration to serve as a self-proclaimed civilian guard to discourage looting at local businesses.

How anyone can look at what happened in Kenosha and the mass shooting at the Oxford High School in Michigan where a 15-year-old killed four other teenagers with a gun purchased by the shooter's father four days prior to the shooting and still maintain that the United States does not have a crisis on its hands, is beyond belief.

A Center for American Progress analysis[xxii] found that the ten states with the weakest gun laws collectively had an aggregate rate of gun violence more than three times higher than the ten states with the strongest gun laws.[56]

We currently have no laws preventing the sale of guns or semi-automatic assault weapons because the majority of Americans believe gun ownership is their birthright. Steven Paddock carried fifty-four suitcases full of guns into a hotel in order to kill concertgoers in Las Vegas. If he had been required to undergo a background check and obtain a license, he may not have had as many guns to shoot. The same could be true about the shooter at Parkland High School. Both shooters had a police record, yet they were still able to purchase guns.

Wayne Robert LaPierre, the chief executive of the NRA, stressed his opposition to a ban on assault weapons by saying that the organization supported efforts to keep weapons out of the hands of the mentally ill. In practice, which would mean every person who plans to purchase a gun would have to have a certificate from a mental health professional stating that he or she is not mentally ill and does not pose a danger to society. But mental health professionals do not have the necessary

---

[xxii] Katie Peters, "Release: 50-State Analysis Shows Weak State Gun Laws Linked to More Gun Violence," Center for American Progress, April 3, 2013, https://americanprogress.org/press/release-50-state-analysis-shows-weak-state-gun-laws-linked-to-more-gun-violence/.

tools to assess potentially dangerous behavior unless a person is paranoid and shows persecutory ideas. Consequently, contrary to Mr. LaPierre's suggestion, it is impossible to predict potentially dangerous behavior.

The New York Attorney General filed a law suit to dissolve the gun rights advocacy group (NRA), accusing top executives of illegal self-dealings. It is interesting to note that Mr. LaPierre described one of the trips on a luxury liner "a security retreat" because he was frightened for his safety in the months after a gunman killed twenty children and six educators at Sandy Hook Elementary School in Newtown, Connecticut, in 2012. "I remember getting there going, 'Thank God I'm safe, nobody can get me here.' And that's how it happened. That's why I used it." He reassured his clients that there is no change in the overall direction of NRA, its programs, or its Second Amendment advocacy.[57]

CONTROLLING GUN VIOLENCE

Michael Siegel of Boston University School of Public Health and associates observed a robust correlation between higher levels of gun ownership and higher firearm homicide rates. They found that states with higher rates of gun ownership had disproportionately large numbers of deaths from firearm-related homicides, a finding which confirms the Kellerman study cited above.[58]

In Missouri, the state legislature repealed its licensing requirements (permit to purchase a gun) in 2007. A study found that the change was associated with an increase of between fifty-five to sixty-three homicides in each of the five years following the repeal. Permit-to-purchase laws reduce the secondhand market for gun sale. These laws require people to get pre-checked by state or local authorities, who then issue a permit allowing a gun purchase. Permit-to-purchase laws make it a crime for anyone to sell or give a gun to someone without a permit.

In 1993, the state of Virginia enacted a one-handgun-a-month law, which resulted in a reduction in the number of criminal firearms sent to nearby states. Few states provide other states a list of people who are banned from buying a gun. Anyone could purchase a gun in another state and bring it home. All loopholes must be removed.

Federal law says if it takes more than three business days for a background check, the sale can proceed without the background checks. As a result, thousands of people who should not have access to guns get them. Dylan Roof, who killed nine people in Charleston, South Carolina in 2015, purchased a gun thanks to this loophole.[59,60]

The Rand Corporation analyzed policies related to gun laws and found that background checks may decrease violent crime and that prohibitions on gun sales to the mentally ill may decrease suicide by guns. Concealed-carry weapons and stand-your-ground laws, on the other hand, increase violent crime. A ban on the sale of assault weapons and high-capacity magazines does reduce mass murders, and minimum age requirements and waiting periods were found to decrease suicide by guns.[61]

Corporate America has spoken in favor of strong measures for gun control. CEOs of many companies, including Levi Strauss, Twitter, and Uber, have stated that they felt a sense of "responsibility and obligation to stand up for the safety of our employees, customers and all Americans in the communities we serve."

Dick's Sporting Goods overhauled its gun sales policies, stopped selling guns in two hundred of its new stores, and destroyed about $5 million worth of weapons, turning them into scrap metal. Dick's also pulled all military-style weapons from its stores, banned high-capacity magazines. and does not sell firearms to people younger than twenty-one. Edward Stack, CEO of Dick's, publicly criticized Senate Majority Leader Mitch McConnell for holding up gun control legislation in Congress. Not surprisingly, the NRA, Republican lawmakers, and customers have chastised Stack for his sensible decisions. Mr. Stack sets an example by not following the greed of other gun sellers and, thereby, saving lives.[62]

The American Medical Societies' Recommendations

In 2015, the American College of Physicians joined the American College of Surgeons, the American College of Obstetricians and Gynecologists, the American Public Health Association, the American Psychiatric Association, the American Academy of Family Physicians, the American Academy of Pediatrics, the American College of Emergency Physicians, and the American Bar Association in a call to action to address gun violence as a public health threat. Fifty-two other organizations subsequently endorsed their call. Their recommendations included encouraging physicians to discuss with their patients the risks associated with having a firearm in the home and to recommend ways to mitigate such risks. They also strongly recommended that the sale of firearms be subject to proof of satisfactory completion of an educational program on firearm safety along with universal background checks to keep guns out of the hands of felons, persons with mental illness, persons with substance use disorders, domestic violence offenders, and others who are prohibited from owning guns.

Other recommendations include banning assault weapons with large-capacity magazines and closing the gun show loophole, which refers to private sales at gun shows, and prosecuting people who sell firearms illegally or purchase firearms for those who are banned from gun possession (straw purchases).[63]

There is a clear need of public education about gun violence, the obsession of gun ownership in this highly civilized society, reviewing the laws related to sales of guns, loopholes in existing laws, and a need to implement a nationwide gun licensing system.

There are serious problems with gun laws in this country. Some members of Congress are committed to change, but the majority of lawmakers who are supported by NRA do not support change. They overlook loopholes and inconsistences in our firearms laws. For example, a young man cannot buy a handgun until he is twenty-one years old, but he can buy an assault-style rifle at the age of eighteen. A person can buy a gun on the internet without a background check in whatever state the seller is located. What is the point of enforcing background checks unless internet and interstate sales are subject to them, too?

Training and licensing for the gun owners significantly reduces the incident of death by gun use. In Connecticut, after state lawmakers required people to obtain a license and safety training for a gun, there was a drop in both gun homicides and suicides.

CONCLUSION

Gun violence in America is unique, not because of our culture, but because we legally possess assault weapons that can kill many people very quickly. After each mass shooting, there is massive media coverage and scores of papers published demanding stronger laws related to gun sales. Democrats propose multiple gun-control measures (common-sense measures), such as strengthening background checks, limiting handgun purchases to one per month, and allowing localities to regulate guns in public buildings to reduce fatalities from gun violence.

Each year, Republican majorities in one or both chambers of the legislature vote them down. GOP legislators say their goal is never to infringe on the people's Second Amendment rights, "Gun control does not save lives. It endangers innocent life by making it harder for good people to defend themselves."[xxiii]

During the last four to five decades, the same scenario repeated itself – no laws passed to curtail gun sales. In fact, the NRA not only succeeded in blocking laws, but they also

---

xxiii Robert McArtney, Washington Post, accessed at http://www.adamebbin.com/news-clips/virginia-republicans-blocked-law-ban-sales-gun-parts-used-mass-shooting

successfully introduced laws prohibiting research to find ways to reduce the epidemic of gun violence, which takes forty thousand lives each year in the United States.

The basic reason for high incidents of gun violence is the American public's obsession to possess guns. As I mentioned earlier, this obsession of self-protection by owning a gun has been going on for the last three to four centuries. It has become extremely difficult to bring a change in this obsessional thinking. No doubt, the NRA is taking full advantage of this pre-occupation with gun possession and promoting gun sales with the least restrictions for monitoring sales. Hundreds of articles and the efforts of numerous organizations have produced very little or no change.

Now that the last presidential election is behind us, I hope laws related to guns become a legislative priority for a nation that, on a daily basis, continues to reel from the havoc brought on by gun violence. We have reason to be cautiously optimistic. President Joseph R. Biden rightfully characterizes gun violence in the United States as a "public health epidemic." In the early 1990s, during his tenure in the U.S. Senate, Biden helped pass the Brady Handgun Violence Prevention Act as well as a ten-year ban on assault weapons and high-capacity magazines in 1994.

It is our (citizens) responsibility to make Americans aware of the consequences of their obsession with guns and very weak laws related to sales of guns. We must ask ourselves, what triggers violent impulses in people to kill indiscriminately? Is there any way we can predict violent behavior in people who purchase guns?

Efforts should be focused on educating people that, in this 21st century, we are living in a highly civilized society with the best police protection in the world. Therefore, we do not need guns for self-protection, except in remote rural areas. People should be able to purchase guns, but not machine guns or a whole arsenal of similar weapons to fight an army.

In order to reduce the number of guns possessed by people and to keep guns out of reach of criminals, dangerous people, and people intending to commit suicide (incomplete sentence) Our knowledge of human behavior is not advanced enough to predict behavior, and we cannot subject every gun buyer to certification from a behavioral scientist in order to buy a gun. Therefore, I am making the following recommendations and implementation to save lives:

1. People should be able to purchase a gun after: Submitting an application for background check, obtaining a license to purchase a gun following training for appropriate use of a gun, safekeeping and waiting for one week.[64]
2. People with a history of mental illness, domestic violence, dementia, alcohol or drug abuse, or a criminal record should not be allowed to purchase a gun.
3. Sales of all automatic guns and silencers should be banned.
4. Open carry laws should be repealed.
5. Gun sales -- online, on Craigslist and eBay, and through private individuals -- should be totally banned.
6. Law enforcement agencies must have tools to track gun trafficking.
7. Law enforcement should be allowed to remove firearms from people deemed potentially violent.
8. There should be no restrictions on research for finding ways to reduce fatalities due to gun violence. There is insufficient data on the underlying reasons for violent deaths due to firearms.

It will most probably take five to ten years to achieve these goals. However, these goals cannot be met unless we educate the people about their obsession with possessing guns.

It is a grueling task and not easy to challenge the NRA, one of the most powerful lobbies in the United States. Their sole purpose is to promote gun sales for profit at the cost of thousands of innocent lives. They control legislators who support their goal of free access to guns for everyone. They take advantage of the American people's obsession with possessing guns. It is similar to the addiction to tobacco and narcotics; we know that people take advantage of this addiction and make millions of dollars at the cost of the suffering and death of people who are addicted to tobacco and narcotics.

I suggest we begin discussion with three groups who have sympathy and empathy regarding the 40,000 gun-related deaths per year in the United States (the highest percentage of any economically developed country)—physicians (health care professionals), educators and clergies (faith leaders). These individuals work closely with their fellow human beings and can play a significant role in educating the public about the dangers of guns and the traumatic effect they have on hundreds and thousands of survivors of gun violence. They can explain that in the last four hundred years, America has changed from being the Wild West to being the most civilized country in the world.

Public education is the best way we have to change behavior. I strongly encourage physicians, clergy, and teachers to take responsibility for educating the public about the dangers of owning a gun, the impact they have on innocent victims, and the traumatic effects gun violence has on thousands of survivors. Physicians, teachers, and clergy should be able to discuss the risks of firearms, particularly the risk to children. They should screen and counsel on the importance of firearm safety and emphasize that no one needs an arsenal of weapons for self-defense.

These three groups—health professionals, faith leaders, and schools and colleges—have access to most people living in

United States, and they are compassionate, care for and value human life, and are concerned about the high incidence of death from gun violence.

I strongly recommend that all organizations such as **Everytown for Gun Safety, The Brady Campaign, Newtown Action Alliance, Americans For Responsible Solutions, and States United to Prevent Gun Violence** that support gun control add a robust public education component to their mission. I am confident we can control the epidemic of gun violence if we intervene early in a young person's life by insisting health professions, faith leaders, and teachers do their part to challenge the unexamined assumptions that for too long have governed the rationale for gun ownership in America.

REFERENCES

1. Williams, Timothy, and Farah Stockman. "Gunman Kills 9 in Dayton Entertainment District." *The New York Times*, August 4, 2019. https://www.nytimes.com/2019/08/04/us/dayton-ohio-shooting.html.

2. Collins, Keith, and David Yaffe-bellany. "About 2 Million Guns Were Sold in the U.S. as Virus Fears Spread." *The New York Times*, April 2, 2020. https://www.nytimes.com/interactive/2020/04/01/business/coronavirus-gun-sales.html.

3. Capehart, Jonathan. "Opinion | Trump Can't Decry Racism and White Supremacy If He Is Their Chief Promoter." *The Washington Post*. WP Company, August 5, 2019. https://www.washingtonpost.com/opinions/2019/08/05/trump-cant-decry-racism-white-supremacy-if-he-is-their-chief-promoter/.

4. Williamson, Marianne. "Opinion | Marianne Williamson: America Doesn't Just Have a Gun Crisis. It Has a Culture Crisis." *The Washington Post*. WP Company, September 3, 2019. https://www.washingtonpost.com/opinions/2019/09/02/marianne-williamson-us-needs-department-peace/.

5. Ingraham, Christopher. "Analysis | There Are More Guns than People in the United States, According to a New Study of Global Firearm Ownership." *The Washington Post*. WP Company, April 27, 2019. https://www.washingtonpost.com/news/wonk/wp/2018/06/19/there-are-more-guns-than-people-in-the-united-states-according-to-a-new-study-of-global-firearm-ownership/.

6. "Gun Ownership." *Wikipedia*. Wikimedia Foundation, November 17, 2021. https://en.wikipedia.org/wiki/Gun_ownership.

7. Neely, Paula. "Jamestown Colonists Resorted to Cannibalism." Science. *National Geographic*, May 3, 2021. https://www.nationalgeographic.com/science/article/130501-jamestown-cannibalism-archeology-science.

8. Rubinkam, Michael. "Worshippers Clutching AR-15 Rifles Hold Commitment Ceremony." *USA Today*. Gannett Satellite Information Network, March 1, 2018. https://www.usatoday.com/story/news/nation/2018/02/28/pennsylvania-church-ceremony-guns/383815002/.

9. Carroll, Lauren. "At DNC, Sen. Chris Murphy Says 90% of Americans Want Expanded Background Checks for Gun Purchases." Politifact. The Poynter Institute. Accessed November 24, 2021. https://www.politifact.com/factchecks/2016/jul/27/chris-murphy/dnc-sen-chris-murphy-says-90-americans-want-expand/.

10. Igielnik, Ruth, and Anna Brown. "Americans' Views on Guns and Gun Ownership: 8 Key Findings." Pew Research Center, May 30, 2020. https://www.pewresearch.org/fact-tank/2017/06/22/key-takeaways-on-americans-views-of-guns-and-gun-ownership/.

11. "WISQARS (Web-Based Injury Statistics Query and Reporting System)." Centers for Disease Control and Prevention, July 1, 2020. https://www.cdc.gov/injury/wisqars/index.html.

12. Grinshteyn, Erin, and David Hemenway. "Violent Death Rates in the U.S. Compared to Those of the Other High-Income Countries, 2015." Preventive Medicine. U.S. National Library of Medicine. Accessed November 24, 2021. https://pubmed.ncbi.nlm.nih.gov/30817955/.

13. Anglemyer, Andrew, Tara Horvath, and George Rutherford. "The Accessibility of Firearms and Risk for Suicide and Homicide Victimization among Household Members." *Annals of Internal Medicine* 160, no. 2 (2014): 101–10. https://doi.org/10.7326/m13-1301.

14. Miller, Matthew, Deborah Azrael, and Catherine Barber. "Suicide Mortality in the United States: The Importance of Attending to Method in Understanding Population-Level Disparities in the Burden of Suicide." *Annual Review of Public Health* 33, no. 1 (2012): 393–408. https://doi.org/10.1146/annurev-publhealth-031811-124636.

15. Aizenman, Nurith. "Gun Violence Deaths: How the U.S. Compares with the Rest of the World." Goats and Soda: Stories of Life in a Changing World. NPR, March 24, 2021. https://www.npr.org/sections/goatsandsoda/2021/03/24/980838151/gun-violence-deaths-how-the-u-s-compares-to-the-rest-of-the-world.

16. Rozsa, Lori, Kayla Epstein, Katie Mettler, and Lindsey Bever. "Parkland Community 'Shocked' after Student's Suicide - the Second in a Week, Officials Say." *The Washington Post*, March 25, 2019. https://www.washingtonpost.com/nation/2019/03/24/parkland-student-dies-apparent-suicide-police-say/.

17. Lopez, German. "America Is One of 6 Countries That Make up More than Half of Gun Deaths Worldwide." Vox, August 29, 2018. https://www.vox.com/2018/8/29/17792776/us-gun-deaths-global.

18. Hodges, Dan. "In Retrospect Sandy Hook Marked the End of the U.S. Gun Control Debate. Once America

Decided Killing Children Was Bearable, It Was over." Twitter, June 19, 2015. https://twitter.com/dpjhodges/status/611943312401002496.

19. Kristof, Nicholas. "New Zealand Shows the U.S. What Leadership Looks Like." *The New York Times*, March 20, 2019. https://www.nytimes.com/2019/03/20/opinion/new-zealand-gun-control.html.

20. Friedman, Richard A. "Why Mass Murderers May Not Be Very Different from You or Me." *The New York Times*, August 8, 2019. https://www.nytimes.com/2019/08/08/opinion/mass-shootings-mental-health.html.

21. Ibid.

22. Swanson, Jeffrey W. "Redirecting the Mental Health and Gun Violence Conversation from Mass Shootings to Suicide." *Psychiatric Services* 69, no. 12 (2018): 1198–99. https://doi.org/10.1176/appi.ps.201800365.

23. Bailey, Issac. "Why Today's Everyday Hate Feels Different to Me." CNN. Cable News Network, July 12, 2018. https://edition.cnn.com/2018/07/11/opinions/mexican-man-attacked-puerto-rico-shirt-bailey-opinion/index.html.

24. Roznovsky, Nicholas. "UCSF Experts: Focus on Mental Illness as Cause of Mass Shootings Is Unfounded and Potentially Harmful." UCSF Department of Psychiatry and Behavioral Sciences, February 28, 2018. https://psychiatry.ucsf.edu/news/ucsf-experts-focus-mental-illness-cause-mass-shootings-unfounded-and-potentially-harmful.

25. "Blaming Mass Shootings on Serious Mental Illness Has Harmful Effects, Says APA Past President." Psychiatric News Alert, February 28, 2018. https://alert.psychnews.org/2018/02/blaming-mass-shootings-on-serious.html.

26. Kessler, Ronald C., Sergio Aguilar-Gaxiola, Jordi Alonso, Somnath Chatterji, Sing Lee, Johan Ormel, T. Bedirhan Üstün, and Philip S. Wang. "The Global Burden of Mental Disorders: An Update from The Who World Mental Health

(WMH) Surveys." *Epidemiologia e Psichiatria Sociale* 18, no. 1 (2009): 23–33. https://doi.org/10.1017/s1121189x00001421.

27. " Reducing Suicides by Firearms." American Public Health Association, November 13, 2018. https://www.apha.org/policies-and-advocacy/public-health-policy-statements/policy-database/2019/01/28/reducing-suicides-by-firearms.

28. Institute of Medicine (U.S.) Committee on Pathophysiology and Prevention of Adolescent and Adult Suicide. "Firearm Availability and Suicide." *Suicide Prevention and Intervention: Summary of a Workshop*. Washington (DC): National Academies Press (U.S.), 2001. https://www.ncbi.nlm.nih.gov/books/NBK223849/.

29. Fox, Maggie. "State-by-State Study Links Gun Ownership with Youth Suicide." NBC News. NBCUniversal News Group, January 17, 2019. https://www.nbcnews.com/health/health-news/state-state-study-links-gun-ownership-youth-suicide-n959946.

30. "Guns and Suicide: A Fatal Link." Harvard T.H. Chan School of Public Health, April 23, 2014. https://www.hsph.harvard.edu/news/magazine/guns-and-suicide.

31. "The Relationship between Firearm Availability and Suicide." RAND Corporation, March 2, 2018. https://www.rand.org/research/gun-policy/analysis/essays/firearm-availability-suicide.html.

32. Miller, Kathy. "Gun Ownership and Older Adults — When Is It Time to Take Action?" *Today's Geriatric Medicine* 12, no. 3, May 2019.

33. Grinshteyn, Erin, and David Hemenway. "Violent Death Rates in the U.S. Compared to Those of the Other High-Income Countries, 2015." *Preventive Medicine* 123 (2019): 20–26. https://doi.org/10.1016/j.ypmed.2019.02.026.

34. Campbell, Jacquelyn C., Daniel Webster, Jane Koziol-McLain, Carolyn Block, Doris Campbell, Mary Ann Curry, Faye Gary, et al. "Risk Factors for Femicide in Abusive

Relationships: Results from a Multisite Case Control Study." *American Journal of Public Health* 93, no. 7 (2003): 1089–97. https://doi.org/10.2105/ajph.93.7.1089.

35. Sorenson, Susan B., and Rebecca A. Schut. "Nonfatal Gun Use in Intimate Partner Violence: A Systematic Review of the Literature." *Trauma, Violence, & Abuse* 19, no. 4 (2016): 431–42. https://doi.org/10.1177/1524838016668589.

36. "Hidden Camera Experiment: Young Kids Drawn to Guns." ABC News. ABC News Internet Ventures, 2014. https://abcnews.go.com/WNT/video/hidden-camera-experiment-children-drawn-guns-found-classroom-22258370.

37. Healy, Melissa. "More than Half of U.S. Gun Owners Store at Least One Firearm without Any Locks, Survey Reveals." *Los Angeles Times*, February 23, 2018. https://www.latimes.com/science/sciencenow/la-sci-sn-safe-gun-storage-20180223-story.html.

38. Carroll, Aaron E. "The Potentially Lifesaving Difference in How a Gun Is Stored." *The New York Times*, May 13, 2019. https://www.nytimes.com/2019/05/13/upshot/gun-safety-children-storage.html.

39. Groetzinger, Kate. "With Accidental Gun Deaths on the Rise, Some Texas Lawmakers Won't Even Support a Gun Safety Public Awareness Campaign." *The Texas Observer*, April 16, 2019. https://www.texasobserver.org/with-accidental-gun-deaths-on-the-rise-some-texas-lawmakers-wont-even-support-a-gun-safety-public-awareness-campaign/.

40. Moran, Mark. "Survey Finds Parents of at-Risk Kids Don't Safely Store Guns." *Psychiatric News* 53, no. 7 (2018). https://doi.org/10.1176/appi.pn.2018.4a10.

41. Gebelhoff, Robert. "Opinion | Opponents of Gun Reforms Say Nothing Can Be Done. Science Says They're Wrong." *The Washington Post*. WP Company, March 23, 2018. https://www.washingtonpost.com/graphics/2018/opinions/gun-control-that-works/.

42. Stevens, John Paul. "The Five Extra Words That Can Fix the Second Amendment." *The Washington Post*. WP Company, April 11, 2014. https://www.washingtonpost.com/opinions/the-five-extra-words-that-can-fix-the-second-amendment/2014/04/11/f8a19578-b8fa-11e3-96ae-f2c36d2b1245_story.html.

43. Yuhas, Alan. "The Right to Bear Arms: What Does the Second Amendment Really Mean?" *The Guardian*, October 5, 2017. https://www.theguardian.com/us-news/2017/oct/05/second-amendment-right-to-bear-arms-meaning-history.

44. Tom, McCarthy. "Gun Safety Groups Not Convinced by Retired Justice's Call to Repeal Second Amendment." *The Guardian*. Guardian News and Media, March 27, 2018. https://www.theguardian.com/law/2018/mar/27/john-paul-stevens-former-supreme-court-justice-repeal-second-amendment.

45. Thrush, Glenn. "Inside Missouri's '2nd Amendment Sanctuary' Fight." *The New York Times*, September 9, 2021. https://www.nytimes.com/2021/09/09/us/politics/missouri-gun-law.html.

46. Gerney, Arkadi, Winnie Stachelberg, and Chelsea Parsons. "Blindfolded, and with One Hand Tied behind the Back." Center for American Progress, April 2, 2013. https://americanprogress.org/article/blindfolded-and-with-one-hand-tied-behind-the-back/.

47. Kaplan, Sheila. "Congress Quashed Research into Gun Violence. since Then, 600,000 People Have Been Shot." *The New York Times*, March 12, 2018. https://www.nytimes.com/2018/03/12/health/gun-violence-research-cdc.html.

48. An Act to amend title 18, United States Code, to provide for better control of the interstate traffic in firearms, Public Law 90-618, 82 Stat. 1213 (1968). https://www.govinfo.gov/content/pkg/STATUTE-82/pdf/STATUTE-82-Pg1213-2.pdf

49. The Omnibus Consolidated Appropriations Act of 1997, Relating to a National Repository for Arson and Explosives Information. Public Law 104–208 (1996). https://www.govinfo.gov/content/pkg/PLAW-104publ208/pdf/PLAW-104publ208.pdf

50. National Research Council, Division of Behavioral and Social Sciences and Education, Committee on Law and Justice, Institute of Medicine, Executive Office, and Committee on Priorities for a Public Health Research Agenda to Reduce the Threat of Firearm-Related Violence. *Priorities for Research to Reduce the Threat of Firearm-Related Violence.* Edited by Patrick W Kelley, Margaret A McCoy, Arlene F Lee, Bruce M Altevogt, and Alan I Leshner. National Academies Press, 2013.

51. Kellermann, Arthur L., and Frederick P. Rivara. "Silencing the Science on Gun Research." *JAMA* 309, no. 6 (2013): 549. https://doi.org/10.1001/jama.2012.208207.

52. Spaulding, Stephen, and Jesse Littlewood. "Power Shift - How People Can Take on the NRA." Common Cause, September 13, 2018. https://www.commoncause.org/resource/powershift-how-people-can-take-on-the-nra/.

53. Stark, David E., and Nigam H. Shah. "Funding and Publication of Research on Gun Violence and Other Leading Causes of Death." *JAMA* 317, no. 1 (2017): 84. https://doi.org/10.1001/jama.2016.16215.

54. Feinblatt, John. "Opinion | in Virginia, Republican Lawmakers Chose the NRA over Public Safety. in November, the Choice Will Lie with Voters." *The Washington Post.* WP Company, July 9, 2019. https://www.washingtonpost.com/opinions/2019/07/09/virginia-republican-lawmakers-chose-nra-over-public-safety-november-choice-will-lie-with-voters/.

55. "The Victims of the Virginia Beach Mass Shooting." *The Washington Post.* WP Company, June 3, 2019. https://www.

washingtonpost.com/graphics/2019/local/virginia-beach-shooting-victims/.

56. Parsons, Chelsea, and Ed Chung. "Opinion | the Virginia Special Session on Gun Legislation Doesn't Have to Be a Farce." *The Washington Post*. WP Company, July 8, 2019. https://www.washingtonpost.com/opinions/2019/07/08/virginia-special-session-gun-legislation-doesnt-have-be-farce/.

57. Gregorian, Dareh. "NRA Bankruptcy Filing Blocked by Texas Judge, Forcing Group to Face New York AG's Lawsuit." NBC News. NBC Universal News Group, May 11, 2021. https://www.nbcnews.com/politics/politics-news/nra-bankruptcy-filing-blocked-texas-judge-forcing-group-face-new-n1267035.

58. Siegel, Michael, Craig S. Ross, and Charles King. "The Relationship between Gun Ownership and Firearm Homicide Rates in the United States, 1981–2010." *American Journal of Public Health* 103, no. 11 (2013): 2098–2105. https://doi.org/10.2105/ajph.2013.301409.

59. "GAO-16-483-Gun Control: Analyzing Available Data Could Help Improve Background Checks Involving Domestic Violence Records." U.S. Government Accountability Office, 2016. https://www.gao.gov/assets/gao-16-483.pdf.

60. Borden, Jeremy. "One Year Later, and the Loophole That Let the Charleston Shooter Buy Guns Is Still Open." The Trace, September 9, 2020. https://www.thetrace.org/2016/06/one-year-later-and-the-loophole-that-let-the-charleston-shooter-buy-his-gun-remains-wide-open/.

61. "The Effects of Child-Access Prevention Laws." RAND Corporation, March 2, 2018. https://www.rand.org/research/gun-policy/analysis/child-access-prevention.html.

62. Siegel, Rachel. "Dick's Sporting Goods CEO Says Overhauled Gun Policies Cost the Company a Quarter of a Billion Dollars." *The Philadelphia Inquirer*, October 8, 2019.

https://www.inquirer.com/business/dicks-sporting-goods-gun-sales-20191008.html.

63. Butkus, Renee, Robert Doherty, and Sue S. Bornstein. "Reducing Firearm Injuries and Deaths in the United States: A Position Paper from the American College of Physicians." *Annals of Internal Medicine* 169, no. 10 (2018): 704. https://doi.org/10.7326/m18-1530.

64. Miller, Matthew, Lisa Hepburn, and Deborah Azrael. "Firearm Acquisition without Background Checks." *Annals of Internal Medicine* 166, no. 4 (2017): 233. https://doi.org/10.7326/m16-1590.

www.ingramcontent.com/pod-product-compliance
Lightning Source LLC
LaVergne TN
LVHW041538060526
838200LV00037B/1044